Diabetic Smoothie Recipe Book

Diabetic Green Smoothie Recipes for Weight Loss and Blood Sugar Detox!

Healthy Diabetic Smoothie Diet

by

Viktoria McCartney

Text Copyright © [Viktoria McCartney]

Table of Contents

Introduction

Smoothies for diabetic patients! In this ultimate smoothie book, the author whips up nutrient-rich recipes using the world's most antioxidant, vitamin and mineral -rich foods, and offers smoothies that are incredibly nutritious and delicious. Readers reported that these smoothie recipes not only helped them to shed pounds but also helped them to think clearly, sleep better, and improve overall health.

Whatever your health goals, fitness regimen, or daily routine, this diabetic smoothie recipe book has perfect smoothies for every occasion. In this comprehensive smoothie book, the author presents a great variety of healthy smoothies that are perfect for diabetic patients. These smoothie recipes are filling and healthy and your body will also thank you for drinking them as your health and energy levels improve. This book includes recipes for solely vegetable smoothies, and solely fruit-based juices, as well as a variety that combine vegetables and fruits.

Throughout this book, the emphasis is put on providing a wide range of flavors, and nutrients.

These diabetic-friendly, whole-food smoothie recipes offer amazing health benefits, from losing weight to boosting energy. Whether you are just starting out on your weight loss journey or looking for healthy diabetic smoothies, this smoothie recipe book is the essential next step in continuing your pursuit of a healthier lifestyle.

Nutrient-rich spinach, potassium-rich bananas, free-radical fighting blueberries and every delicious natural ingredient you can think of pairs up in this smoothie book. All recipes are quick and easy and take less than 10 minutes to make. Every recipe contains `sustaining` information to help you plan your meals and meet your dietary needs. Are you ready to look healthier, slimmer, and sexier than you have in years? Then get this book now!

How green smoothies benefit diabetes?

Drinking green smoothies daily may help you to improve your diabetes. Here is how:

1. **Weight loss**: Everyone knows that excess weight is one of the known risk factors for type 2 diabetes. People who do exercise daily and maintain a diet plan are often able to reverse and manage their diabetes. Green smoothies contain vegetables and fruits and are a potent weight loss strategy.

2. **Energy for exercise**: People who exercise daily can effectively manage their diabetes. Daily green smoothie drinkers reveal that green smoothies provide them with more energy for exercise.

3. **Healthier diet**: Green smoothies are a part of a healthier diet. People who drink green smoothies daily consume less processed foods.

4. **Vegetables can help heal the pancreas**: Vegetables such as broccoli and collards are particularly beneficial to the pancreas. You can combine dandelion root, broccoli, kale, collards, and other vegetable and your pancreas will improve if it is not totally destroyed.

Mistakes people make with smoothies for diabetes

When preparing smoothies, people often think fruit + yogurt combination. However, diabetic smoothies contain basically no dairy products, minimal fruit, and low-sugar fruits. Here are some common mistakes people make:

1. **Too much fruit:** When making diabetic smoothies, keep your fruit amount to a minimum or completely avoid fruits if you already developed diabetes.

2. **Including sweeteners:** When you avoid fruits, you may be thinking to add a bit of sugar, but you must avoid all types of sugar. You need to be mindful of any sources of sugar, even natural ones like agave, maple syrup, and honey. Also, avoid artificial sweeteners like NutraSweet, Truvia, and Splenda. They can cause side effects such as altering the gut bacteria and others. Also, avoid sugar alcohols such as xylitol, sorbitol, and erythritol. Try a few drops of monk fruit or liquid stevia in your smoothies. One trick to add sweetener to your smoothies is to add a high-quality protein powder that is sweetened with monk fruit or stevia.

3. **Not including fat or fiber:** Ideally, you should use fiber-rich vegetables and fruits that will help slow down the release of glucose into the bloodstream. Including fat into your smoothies is another good idea. Fat keeps you full for longer. Include good fats such as coconut, avocado (and their oils), nuts, seeds, nut and seed butter and oils.

4. **Not checking blood sugar:** Keep an eye on your sugar level before and after you drink your smoothie. This will help you understand how certain ingredients affect your glucose levels and you can include or avoid ingredients in the future.

Which nutrients in vegetables help diabetes?

You should try to include these nutrients in your smoothie:

1. **Chromium:** This ingredient is an important part of your diabetic management. Enough chromium prevents glucose being stored as body fat in the body. On the other hand, a deficiency of chromium can lead to diabetes and hypoglycemia. Ingredients that contain chromium include bananas, oranges, basil, grapes, apples, and romaine lettuce.

2. **Sulfur:** Sulfur determines how insulin is produced in the body. Sulfur deficiency can heighten your risk of developing diabetes. Food like nuts, watermelon, apricots, peaches, sweet potatoes, bok choy, avocado, cabbage, and kale contain much-needed sulfur.

3. **Vanadium:** Vanadium is another ingredient that can help you fight diabetes. You need to get a variety of mineral-rich vegetables, fruits, and legumes in your diet. Vanadium helps you control blood sugar and can be found in spinach, parsley, and oats.

4. **Probiotics:** Poor gut health can heighten your risk of developing diabetes. Incorporate fermented foods to boost good bacteria in your gut. Include fermented foods such as homemade kombucha, unsweetened kefir, yogurt, and fermented coconut water in your smoothies.

Some of the alarming diabetic statistics

1. Diabetes is the 7th leading cause of death in the U.S.
2. Every year, 1.5 million Americans are diagnosed with diabetes.
3. Diabetes is the costliest chronic illness. This disease costs Americans $327 billion in 2017 alone.

Green Smoothie Recipes

Weight Loss Smoothies

1. Five Ingredient Green Smoothie

This recipe is going to give you an energy boost in the morning.

Prep time: 5 minutes	Servings: 2

Ingredients

- o   Ice – 1 cup

- o   Fresh or frozen banana, apple, mango or pineapple – 1 cup

- o   Spinach or greens of your choice- 2 handfuls

- o   Avocado – ½

- Unsweetened almond milk or coconut milk – 1 to 1 ½ cups

- Protein powder – 2 scoops

- MCT oil – 1 tsp.

Method

1. Place all the ingredients in a blender.
2. Blend until smooth and enjoy.

Nutritional Facts Per Serving

- Calories: 215

- Fat: 8g

- Carb: 22.5g

- Protein: 13g

2. Peaches and Cream Oatmeal Smoothie

This is a weight loss breakfast smoothie

Prep time: 5 minutes	Servings: 1

Ingredients

- o Frozen peach slices – 1 cup

- o Greek yogurt – 1 cup

- o Oatmeal – ¼ cup

- o Vanilla extract – ¼ tsp.

- o Almond milk – 1 cup

Method

1. Combine everything in a blender and blend until smooth.
2. Serve.

Nutritional Facts Per Serving

- o Calories: 331

- Fat: 4g
- Carb: 46g
- Protein: 29g

3. Superfood Smoothie

This weight loss smoothie is packed with ingredients that are good for your health.

Prep time: 2 minutes	Servings: 1

Ingredients

- o Frozen banana – ½

- o Frozen mixed berries – 1 cup

- o Fresh spinach – 1 cup

- o Chia seeds – 1 Tbsp.

- o Ground flax – 1 Tbsp.

- o Almond butter – 1 Tbsp.

- o Unsweetened almond milk – 1 cup

Method

1. Combine everything in a blender and blend until smooth.
2. Serve.

Nutritional Facts Per Serving

- Calories: 368

- Fat: 19g

- Carb: 58g

- Protein: 12g

4. Sprig of Parsley

The combination of watercress, chia, and parsley gives you a fat-fighting drink.

Prep time: 2 minutes	Servings: 3

Ingredients

- Fresh parsley -1/4 cup (including the stems)
- Watercress – ½ cup
- Frozen strawberries – ½ cup
- Frozen banana – ½
- Chia seeds – 1 tsp.
- Plant-based protein powder – 1 scoop
- Water to blend

Method

1. Blend everything in a blender.
2. Serve.

Nutritional Facts Per Serving

- Calories: 214

- Fat: 2g
- Carb: 22g
- Protein: 28.5g

5. Romaine Around

Romaine Lettuce is one of the most nutritious vegetables and helps you to lose weight.

Prep time: 5 minutes	Servings: 1

Ingredients

- o   Romaine lettuce – 1 cup

- o   Spinach – ½ cup

- o   Apple – ½, peeled and quartered

- o   Chia seeds – 1 Tbsp.

- o   Unsweetened almond milk – ½ cup

- o   Plain plant-based protein powder – 1 scoop

- o   Water to blend

Method

1. Blend everything in the blender and serve.

Nutritional Facts Per Serving

- Calories: 280

- Fat: 5.8g

- Carb: 27g

- Protein: 20g

Detox and Cleansing Smoothies

6. Green Detox Smoothie

This is a detox smoothie recipe with great taste.

Prep time: 10 minutes	Servings: 4

Ingredients

- o   Baby spinach – 2 cups

- o   Baby kale – 2 cups

- o   Celery – 2 ribs, chopped

- o   Green apple – 1, medium, chopped

- o   Frozen sliced banana – 1 cup

- o   Almond milk -1 cup

- o Grated fresh ginger -1 Tbsp.

- o Chia seeds – 1 Tbsp.

- o Honey – 1 Tbsp.

Method

1. Combine everything in a blender and blend until smooth.
2. Serve.

Nutritional Facts Per Serving

- o Calories: 136

- o Fat: 1g

- o Carb: 28g

- o Protein: 1g

7. Cucumber Ginger Detox

Superfood spinach, hydrating cucumber, and spicy ginger, all are good for the digestive system and to fight inflammation.

Prep time: 5 minutes	Servings: 2

Ingredients

- o   Spinach – 1 ½ oz.

- o   Orange – 1, peeled

- o   Ginger – ½ inch, peeled

- o   Water – 1 cup

- o   Cucumber – 1, chopped

- o   Avocado – ½ chopped

- o   Ice – 1 cup

- o   Rosehips – 1 tsp.

Method

1. Combine everything in the blender and blend until smooth.
2. Serve.

Nutritional Facts Per Serving

o   Calories: 144

o   Fat: 8g

o   Carb: 20g

o   Protein: 3g

8. Green Protein Smoothie Recipe

Filled with anti-inflammatory and antioxidant properties, this detox drink tastes like a dream.

Prep time: 5 minutes	Servings: 2

Ingredients

- o Kale – 1 oz.

- o Pineapple – 4 oz.

- o Pea protein – 1 Tbsp.

- o Water – 1 cup

- o Tangerine – 1, peeled

- o Avocado – ½

- o Almonds – 3 Tbsp.

- o Ice – 1 cup

Method

1. Except for the almonds, blend everything in the blender.
2. Top with almonds and serve.

Nutritional Facts Per Serving

- o   Calories: 227

- o   Fat: 15g

- o   Carb: 21g

- o   Protein: 7g

9. Ginger Detox Twist

If the traditional detox drinks are too harsh for your stomach, then try this smoothie.

Prep time: 5 minutes	Servings: 2

Ingredients

- o Collard greens – 1 ½ oz.

- o Apple – 1 chopped

- o Ginger – ½ inch

- o Water – 1 cup

- o Persian cucumbers – 2, chopped

- o Meyer lemon – 1, peeled

- o Chlorella – ½ tsp.

- o Ice – 1 cup

Method

1. Blend everything in a blender and serve.

Nutritional Facts Per Serving

- o Calories: 114

- o Fat: 1g

- o Carb: 22g

- o Protein: 5g

10. Classic Apple Detox Smoothie Recipe

Vitamin-rich spinach, apple, hydrating celery, cucumber, alkalizing lemon, and anti-inflammatory ginger makes the perfect detox drink.

Prep time: 5 minutes	Servings: 2

Ingredients

- o   Baby spinach – 1 ½ oz.

- o   Celery – 2 oz. chopped

- o   Lemon – 1, juiced

- o   Water – 1 cup

- o   Apple – 1 chopped

- o   Mini cucumber – 1, chopped

- o   Ginger – ½ inch, peeled and chopped

- o   Ice – 1 cup

Method

1. Blend everything in a blender and enjoy.

Nutritional Facts Per Serving

o   Calories: 66

o   Fat: 0g

o   Carb: 17g

o   Protein: 1g

Antioxidant Smoothies

11. Almond Banana Smoothie

Cinnamon is rich in antioxidants; walnuts have antioxidant and omega-3 fatty acids. Spinach provides calcium, vitamin A, K, and C.

Prep time: 5 minutes	Servings: 2

Ingredients

- o Baby spinach – 1 ½ oz.

- o Rolled oats – 3 Tbsps.

- o Cinnamon – 1 tsp.

- o Ice – 1 cup

- o Bananas – 2, peeled

- o Walnuts – 3 Tbsps.

- o   Almond milk – 1 cup

Method

1. Except for the cinnamon and walnuts, blend everything in the blender.
2. Top with cinnamon and walnuts and serve.

Nutritional Facts Per Serving

- o   Calories: 266
- o   Fat: 10g
- o   Carb: 47g
- o   Protein: 5g

12.   The Energizer

This smoothie provides a high concentration of antioxidants and chlorophyll to fully activate each cell of your body.

Prep time: 5 minutes	Servings: 1

Ingredients

- Kiwi fruits – 2, peeled

- Banana – 1, peeled

- Avocado – 1, peeled and pitted

- Fresh kale leaves – 3 to 4, chopped

- Broccoli – ½ cup

- Matcha powder – 2 tsp.

- Unsweetened almond milk – ½ cup

- Tahini – 1 Tbsp.

Method

1. Process the ingredients into a blender.
2. Serve.

Nutritional Facts Per Serving

- Calories: 356

- Fat: 21g

- Carb: 40g

- Protein: 8.3g

13.   Smoothie Verde

Apple used in the recipes provides antioxidants. Tomatillos and lime provide a high amount of vitamin C.

Prep time: 5 minutes	Servings: 2

Ingredients

- Collard greens – 1 ½ oz.

- Tomatillos – 2, husked

- Pea protein – 1 Tbsp.

- Ice – 1 cup

- Apple – 1, chopped

- Lime – 1 juiced

- Water – 1 cup

Method

1. Blend everything in a blender and serve.

Nutritional Facts Per Serving

- Calories: 90

- Fat: 0g

- Carb: 18g

- Protein: 6g

14.   Kumquat Tart Smoothie

This smoothie offers a great combination of antioxidants and vitamins.

Prep time: 5 minutes	Servings: 2

Ingredients

- o Swiss chard – 1 ½ oz.

- o Pineapple – 4 oz.

- o Hemp seeds – 1 Tbsp.

- o Ice – 1 cup

- o Pear – 1, chopped

- o Kumquats – 2 oz.

- o Water -1 cup

Method

1. Blend everything in a blender and serve.

Nutritional Facts Per Serving

- Calories: 123
- Fat: 3g
- Carb: 24g
- Protein: 3g

15.   Pear and Pineapple Smoothie

Pear, pineapple and hemp seeds used in this recipe are rich with antioxidants and lower inflammation.

Prep time: 5 minutes	Servings: 2

Ingredients

- Swiss chard – 1 ½ oz.

- Pineapple – 4 oz.

- Hemp seeds – 1 Tbsp.

- Ice – 1 cup

- Pear – 1 chopped

- Kumquats – 2 oz.

- Water – 1 cup

Method

1. Blend everything in a blender and serve.

40

Nutritional Facts Per Serving

- Calories: 123

- Fat: 3g

- Carb: 24g

- Protein: 3g

Alkalizing Smoothie Recipes

16.   Alkaline Green Smoothie

This alkaline recipe is loaded with fiber, minerals, and vitamins and is really delicious.

Prep time: 10 minutes	Servings: 2

Ingredients

- o   Filtered water or raw coconut water – ¾ cup

- o   Firmly packed baby spinach – 2 cups

- o   Avocado – 1 medium, peeled and pitted

- o   English cucumber – ½, roughly chopped

- o   Finely grated lime zest – 1 tsp.

- o   Liquid stevia – 20 drops, plus more to taste

- o   Pinch of sea salt

- Ice cubes – 2 cups

Method

1. Add everything into the blender and blend until smooth.
2. Serve.

Nutritional Facts Per Serving

- Calories: 293

- Fat: 19.8g

- Carb: 32.9g

- Protein: 4.9g

17.   Minty Alkaline Green Smoothie

The smoothie recipe includes lemons and kiwis and turns alkaline once metabolized.

Prep time: 10 minutes	Servings: 2

Ingredients

- o   Green apple – 1, peeled, and sliced

- o   English cucumber – ½, diced

- o   Spinach – 1 cup, tightly packed

- o   Small handful fresh mint – 10 large leaves

- o   Honey - 2 tsp.

- o   Banana – 1

- o   Water – ¼ cup

- o   Raw coconut oil – 1 Tbsp.

Method

1. Blend everything in a blender and serve.

Nutritional Facts Per Serving

- Calories: 237
- Fat: 7.7g
- Carb: 45.7g
- Protein: 2.8g

18.   Alkalinizing Green Smoothie

The recipe tastes sweet but provides a boost to your immunity with powerful alkalinizing benefits.

| Prep time: 10 minutes | Servings: 1 |

Ingredients

- o   Pomegranate juice – 1 cup

- o   Mango – 1

- o   Wheatgrass – ½ cup, juiced

- o   Flax seeds – 2 Tbsp.

Method

1. Combine everything in a blender and blend until smooth.
2. Serve.

Nutritional Facts Per Serving

- o   Calories: 340

- Fat: 10g
- Carb: 63g
- Protein: 5g

19. Alkaline Green Smoothie

Here is another alkaline green smoothie. Drinking an alkalizing green smoothie is an easy way for your body to get fiber and nutrients.

Prep time: 10 minutes	Servings: 1

Ingredients

- o Cucumber – 1, chopped

- o Kale leaves – 3, torn

- o Fresh mint – 5 stems

- o Fresh parsley – 3 stems

- o Fresh ginger – 1-inch piece

- o Avocado – 1, chopped

- o Coconut water – 1 cup

- ○ Hemp seeds – 2 Tbsp.

- ○ Stevia – 2 to 3 drops

Method

1. Place everything in a blender and blend until smooth.
2. Serve.

Nutritional Facts Per Serving

- ○ Calories: 623

- ○ Fat: 41g

- ○ Carb: 61.3g

- ○ Protein: 17.2g

20.   Green Alkaline Shake

Alkaline smoothie balances any acid in your system and helps ease acid reflux symptoms.

Prep time: 5 minutes	Servings: 1

Ingredients

- o   Coconut water – 1 cup

- o   Kale leaves – 3

- o   Ginger – 1-inch piece

- o   Avocado – ½

- o   Mango chunks – 1/ cup

- o   Ice

Method

1.   Blend everything in a blender and serve.

Nutritional Facts Per Serving

- Calories: 310
- Fat: 20.1g
- Carb: 31.4g
- Protein: 4.6g

Smoothies for Digestive Health

21.   Digestion Smoothie

This green smoothie is packed with immune-boosting and digestion-enhancing foods.

Prep time: 10 minutes	Servings: 2

Ingredients

- o Frozen pineapple chunks – 1 cup

- o Frozen banana – ½

- o Water – ½ cup

- o Coconut water – ½ cup

- o Fresh parsley leaves – ¼ cup

- o Avocado – 2 Tbsp.

- Freshly grated ginger – 1 tsp.

- Probiotic powder – ¼ tsp.

- Lemon or lime slice for garnish

Method

1. Add all the ingredients and blend until smooth.

Nutritional Facts Per Serving

- Calories: 210

- Fat: 3g

- Carb: 47g

- Protein: 3g

22.   Healthy Gut Smoothie

This is a nutrient-rich soothing smoothie. It promotes a healthy gut and heals an unhappy digestive system.

Prep time: 5 minutes	Servings: 1

Ingredients

- o   Plain while milk Kefir – ¾ cup

- o   Non-dairy milk – ¼ cup

- o   Ripe banana – 1 large

- o   Ice cubes – 4

- o   Kale – 2 leaves

- o   Fresh ginger – 2 tsps.

Method

1. Add all the ingredients to the blender and blend until smooth.
2. Serve.

Nutritional Facts Per Serving

- Calories: 319

- Fat: 8.1g

- Carb: 51.1g

- Protein: 13.7g

23.   Gut Healthy Green Smoothie

This is a super fruit smooth and beneficial for your gut health.

Prep time: 5 minutes	Servings: 1

Ingredients

- o   Fresh pineapple – 1 cup, diced

- o   Whole kiwis – 3, skin removed

- o   Cucumber – ½ cup, skinned and chopped

- o   Celery – 1 stalk

- o   Baby spinach – 1 handful

- o   Fresh lime juice – 2 Tbsp.

- o   Coconut water – ½ cup

- o   Organic prebiotic powder – 1 scoop

Method

1. Combine everything in a blender and blend until smooth.

Nutritional Facts Per Serving

- ○ Calories: 296

- ○ Fat: 2.1g

- ○ Carb: 73g

- ○ Protein: 6.9g

24.   Probiotic Green Smoothie

This green smoothie is packed with fiber, healthy fats, and probiotics and keeps your digestive tract healthy and clean.

Prep time: 15 minutes	Servings: 2

Ingredients

- o   Coconut water kefir – 2 cups

- o   Apple – 1, chopped

- o   Pear – 1, chopped

- o   Cucumber – 1 chopped

- o   Spinach – 1 handful

- o   Avocado – ½

- o   Celery – 2 stalks

- Ginger – 1 Tbsp. chopped

- Juice of 1 lemon

- Juice of 1 lime

Method

1. Place everything in a blender and blend until smooth.
2. Serve.

Nutritional Facts Per Serving

- Calories: 287

- Fat: 10.7g

- Carb: 54.9g

- Protein: 3.8g

25.   Gut healthy smoothie

This is another gut healthy smoothie.

Prep time: 5 minutes	Servings: 1

Ingredients

- o Unripe banana – ½

- o Frozen raspberries – ½ cup

- o Unsweetened almond milk – 1 cup

- o Avocado – ¼ cup

- o Plain Greek yogurt – 1/3 cup

- o Ground ginger – 1 tsp.

- o Ice – ½ cup

- o Vanilla protein powder – 1 scoop

Method

1. Blend everything in a blender and serve.

Nutritional Facts Per Serving

- Calories: 491
- Fat: 15.2g
- Carb: 66.6g
- Protein: 29.3g

Fruit free Smoothie

26.   Cucumber Smoothie with Ginger

This ginger-cucumber smoothie is healthy and refreshing.

Prep time: 5 minutes	Servings: 1

Ingredients

- o   Medium cucumber – 1, peeled and sliced

- o   Water – 2 cups

- o   Spinach – 1 cup

- o   Fresh ginger – ½ tsp. peeled and chopped

Method

1. In a blender, add everything and process until smooth.
2. Serve.

Nutritional Facts Per Serving

- Calories: 55
- Fat: 0.5g
- Carb: 12.7g
- Protein: 2.9g

27.   Celery Smoothie

Celery is high in beta-carotene, manganese, and vitamin C. It helps you to lose weight.

Prep time: 5 minutes	Servings: 1

Ingredients

- Celery – 1 stalk, chopped

- Fresh parsley – 1 Tbsp. chopped

- Baby spinach – 1 cup

- Small cucumber – 1, chopped

- Water – 1 cup

- Ice cubes

Method

1. Add all the ingredients in a blender and blend until smooth.
2. Serve.

Nutritional Facts Per Serving

- o Calories: 56

- o Fat: 0.5g

- o Carb: 12.8g

- o Protein: 3.1g

28.   Spinach Smoothie

Spinach is high in vitamins C and K. Vitamin K is good for bone health.

Prep time: 5 minutes	Servings: 1

Ingredients

- o   Spinach – 3 cups

- o   Kale leaves – 1 cup, chopped

- o   Water – 2 cups

- o   Mint leaves to garnish

- o   Ice cubes

- o   Spirulina – 1 tsp.

Method

1. Except for the mint leaves, add everything in a blender and blend until smooth.

2. Garnish with mint leaves and serve.

Nutritional Facts Per Serving

- Calories: 79

- Fat: 1g

- Carb: 12.9g

- Protein: 9g

29. Celery and Romaine Lettuce Smoothie

Romaine lettuce is rich in minerals, vitamins, and antioxidants. Celery is high in magnesium, folic acid, and calcium, vitamins, and potassium.

| Prep time: 5 minutes | Servings: 1 |

Ingredients

- o   Celery – 2 stalks

- o   Romaine lettuce – 3 cups

- o   Baby spinach – 1 cup

- o   Kale – 1 cup

- o   Fennel bulb- ½ cup, shredded

- o   Spirulina – 2 tsps.

- o   Water – 2 cups

- o   Ice cubes

Method

1. Add everything in a blender and blend until smooth.
2. Enjoy.

Nutritional Facts Per Serving

- Calories: 122

- Fat: 1.7g

- Carb: 20.6g

- Protein: 12.4g

30.   Zucchini Smoothie with Fennel

Zucchini is a great source of manganese, fiber, antioxidants, and vitamin C and A. Fennel bulb is high in vitamin C.

Prep time: 5 minutes	Servings: 1

Ingredients

- Fennel bulb – ½ cup, shredded

- Zucchini – 2 cups, peeled and chopped

- Fresh parsley – 5 Tbsps. chopped

- Celery – 2 stalks, chopped

- Small cucumber – 1, chopped

- Water -1 cup

- Ice cubes

- Mint leaves for garnish

Method

1. Except for the mint leaves, add everything in the blender and blend until smooth.
2. Garnish with mint leaves and serve.

Nutritional Facts Per Serving

- Calories: 107

- Fat: 1g

- Carb: 23.9g

- Protein: 6g

Conclusion

With the help of this smoothie book, heal your digestive system, boost your metabolism, and turn off your fat genes for good. Every recipe tastes as good as it looks and fills you up. They are a perfect choice for any meal or midday snack. This book is the fastest and most delicious way to improve health and sip off the pounds! If you want to be happier, have more energy, and feel healthier every single day, this diabetic smoothie book is for you.

Printed in Great Britain
by Amazon